This Book is the Property of

_____

Firearms Collector's Log Book
Captain J. F. C. Adams

FastForwardPublishing.com

ISBN-13: 978-1507787779
ISBN-10: 1507787774

Table of Contents

Introduction

This book has been designed to be an important accessory for anyone who owns firearms. It gives you a record of the important specifics of each of your firearms that will enable quick identification in the event of a theft, fire or other situation. Your collection will be documented so you will have all the information needed for insurance or police.

To effectively use this tool, every time you acquire a firearm, follow the prompts and record the as much of information possible about that firearm. Fill in as much information as possible. There is even space to include a photograph of the firearm if you want to include one -- paste over the light grey "Photo of Firearm". And then update as necessary.

This book contains enough pages for 50 firearms. If your collection is larger (or becomes larger), just get another copy and then keep a set of books (number them as a set of volumes). It is suggested that this book be kept separate from your firearms, perhaps in a safe, safety deposit box or other secure location.

This book was designed for the average owner or collector as tool to document personal property. Although it contains much of the information required for a Federal Firearms License (FLL) and Curio and Relic (C&R) license holders, licensees should refer to Bureau of Alcohol, Tobacco, and Firearms (ATF) regulations to make sure that they are within compliance.

4

Index of Firearms

Firearm 39	Firearm:	Page 84
Firearm 40	Firearm:	Page 86
Firearm 41	Firearm:	Page 88
Firearm 42	Firearm:	Page 90
Firearm 43	Firearm:	Page 92
Firearm 44	Firearm:	Page 94
Firearm 45	Firearm:	Page 96
Firearm 46	Firearm:	Page 98
Firearm 47	Firearm:	Page 100
Firearm 48	Firearm:	Page 102
Firearm 49	Firearm:	Page 104
Firearm 50	Firearm:	Page 106

Insurance Information

Insurance Information	
National Carrier:	
Policy Number:	Phone Number:
Local Insurance Agency:	
Primary Contact:	
Phone:	eMail:
Secondary Contact:	
Phone:	eMail:

Photo of Firearm 1

Manufacturer & Model #:	Serial #:
Type: (circle one) Rifle Shotgun Handgun Other:	
Caliber/Gauge:	Action:
Barrel Length (end to end):	Finish:
Date Purchased:	From:
Price:	Paperwork:
Condition:	
Features:	

Accessories/Repairs		
Date	Description	Cost

Beneficiary:	
Date Sold:	To:
Price:	Phone:
Condition:	Address:

Notes:

Photo of Firearm 2

Manufacturer & Model #:	Serial #:
Type: (circle one) Rifle Shotgun Handgun Other:	
Caliber/Gauge:	Action:
Barrel Length (end to end):	Finish:
Date Purchased:	From:
Price:	Paperwork:
Condition:	
Features:	

Accessories/Repairs		
Date	Description	Cost

Beneficiary:

Date Sold:	To:
Price:	Phone:
Condition:	Address:

Notes:

Photo of Firearm 3

Manufacturer & Model #:	Serial #:
Type: (circle one) Rifle Shotgun Handgun Other:	
Caliber/Gauge:	Action:
Barrel Length (end to end):	Finish:
Date Purchased:	From:
Price:	Paperwork:
Condition:	
Features:	

Accessories/Repairs		
Date	Description	Cost

Beneficiary:

Date Sold:	To:
Price:	Phone:
Condition:	Address:

Notes:

Photo of Firearm 4

Manufacturer & Model #:	Serial #:
Type: (circle one) Rifle Shotgun Handgun Other:	
Caliber/Gauge:	Action:
Barrel Length (end to end):	Finish:
Date Purchased:	From:
Price:	Paperwork:
Condition:	
Features:	

Accessories/Repairs		
Date	Description	Cost

Beneficiary:

Date Sold:	To:
Price:	Phone:
Condition:	Address:

Notes:

Photo of Firearm 5

Manufacturer & Model #:	Serial #:
Type: (circle one) Rifle Shotgun Handgun Other:	
Caliber/Gauge:	Action:
Barrel Length (end to end):	Finish:
Date Purchased:	From:
Price:	Paperwork:
Condition:	
Features:	

Accessories/Repairs		
Date	Description	Cost

Beneficiary:

Date Sold:	To:
Price:	Phone:
Condition:	Address:

Notes:

Photo of Firearm 6

Manufacturer & Model #:	Serial #:
Type: (circle one) Rifle Shotgun Handgun Other:	
Caliber/Gauge:	Action:
Barrel Length (end to end):	Finish:
Date Purchased:	From:
Price:	Paperwork:
Condition:	
Features:	

Accessories/Repairs		
Date	Description	Cost

Beneficiary:	
Date Sold:	To:
Price:	Phone:
Condition:	Address:

Notes:

Photo of Firearm 7

Manufacturer & Model #:	Serial #:
Type: (circle one) Rifle Shotgun Handgun Other:	
Caliber/Gauge:	Action:
Barrel Length (end to end):	Finish:
Date Purchased:	From:
Price:	Paperwork:
Condition:	
Features:	

Accessories/Repairs		
Date	Description	Cost

Beneficiary:	
Date Sold:	To:
Price:	Phone:
Condition:	Address:

Notes:

Photo of Firearm 8

Manufacturer & Model #:	Serial #:
Type: (circle one) Rifle Shotgun Handgun Other:	
Caliber/Gauge:	Action:
Barrel Length (end to end):	Finish:
Date Purchased:	From:
Price:	Paperwork:
Condition:	
Features:	

Accessories/Repairs		
Date	Description	Cost

Beneficiary:

Date Sold:	To:
Price:	Phone:
Condition:	Address:

Notes:

Photo of Firearm 9

Manufacturer & Model #:	Serial #:
Type: (circle one) Rifle Shotgun Handgun Other:	
Caliber/Gauge:	Action:
Barrel Length (end to end):	Finish:
Date Purchased:	From:
Price:	Paperwork:
Condition:	
Features:	

Accessories/Repairs		
Date	Description	Cost

Beneficiary:

Date Sold:	To:
Price:	Phone:
Condition:	Address:

Notes:

Photo of Firearm 10

Manufacturer & Model #:	Serial #:
Type: (circle one) Rifle Shotgun Handgun Other:	
Caliber/Gauge:	Action:
Barrel Length (end to end):	Finish:
Date Purchased:	From:
Price:	Paperwork:
Condition:	
Features:	

Accessories/Repairs		
Date	Description	Cost

Beneficiary:

Date Sold:	To:
Price:	Phone:
Condition:	Address:

Notes:

Photo of Firearm 11

Manufacturer & Model #:	Serial #:
Type: (circle one) Rifle Shotgun Handgun Other:	
Caliber/Gauge:	Action:
Barrel Length (end to end):	Finish:
Date Purchased:	From:
Price:	Paperwork:
Condition:	
Features:	

Accessories/Repairs		
Date	Description	Cost

Beneficiary:		
Date Sold:	To:	
Price:	Phone:	
Condition:	Address:	
Notes:		

Photo of Firearm 12

Manufacturer & Model #:	Serial #:
Type: (circle one) Rifle Shotgun Handgun Other:	
Caliber/Gauge:	Action:
Barrel Length (end to end):	Finish:
Date Purchased:	From:
Price:	Paperwork:
Condition:	
Features:	

31

Accessories/Repairs		
Date	Description	Cost

Beneficiary:

Date Sold:	To:
Price:	Phone:
Condition:	Address:

Notes:

Photo of Firearm 13

Manufacturer & Model #:	Serial #:
Type: (circle one) Rifle Shotgun Handgun Other:	
Caliber/Gauge:	Action:
Barrel Length (end to end):	Finish:
Date Purchased:	From:
Price:	Paperwork:
Condition:	
Features:	

Accessories/Repairs		
Date	Description	Cost

Beneficiary:

Date Sold:	To:
Price:	Phone:
Condition:	Address:

Notes:

Photo of Firearm 14

Manufacturer & Model #:	Serial #:
Type: (circle one) Rifle Shotgun Handgun Other:	
Caliber/Gauge:	Action:
Barrel Length (end to end):	Finish:
Date Purchased:	From:
Price:	Paperwork:
Condition:	
Features:	

Accessories/Repairs		
Date	Description	Cost

Beneficiary:		
Date Sold:	To:	
Price:	Phone:	
Condition:	Address:	
Notes:		

Photo of Firearm 15

Manufacturer & Model #:	Serial #:
Type: (circle one) Rifle Shotgun Handgun Other:	
Caliber/Gauge:	Action:
Barrel Length (end to end):	Finish:
Date Purchased:	From:
Price:	Paperwork:
Condition:	
Features:	

Accessories/Repairs		
Date	Description	Cost

Beneficiary:

Date Sold:	To:
Price:	Phone:
Condition:	Address:

Notes:

Photo of Firearm 16

Manufacturer & Model #:	Serial #:
Type: (circle one) Rifle Shotgun Handgun Other:	
Caliber/Gauge:	Action:
Barrel Length (end to end):	Finish:
Date Purchased:	From:
Price:	Paperwork:
Condition:	
Features:	

Accessories/Repairs		
Date	Description	Cost

Beneficiary:

Date Sold:	To:
Price:	Phone:
Condition:	Address:

Notes:

Photo of Firearm 17

Manufacturer & Model #:	Serial #:
Type: (circle one) Rifle Shotgun Handgun Other:	
Caliber/Gauge:	Action:
Barrel Length (end to end):	Finish:
Date Purchased:	From:
Price:	Paperwork:
Condition:	
Features:	

Accessories/Repairs		
Date	Description	Cost

Beneficiary:	
Date Sold:	To:
Price:	Phone:
Condition:	Address:
Notes:	

Photo of Firearm 18

Manufacturer & Model #:	Serial #:
Type: (circle one) Rifle Shotgun Handgun Other:	
Caliber/Gauge:	Action:
Barrel Length (end to end):	Finish:
Date Purchased:	From:
Price:	Paperwork:
Condition:	
Features:	

Accessories/Repairs		
Date	Description	Cost

Beneficiary:	
Date Sold:	To:
Price:	Phone:
Condition:	Address:

Notes:

Photo of Firearm 19

Manufacturer & Model #:	Serial #:
Type: (circle one) Rifle Shotgun Handgun Other:	
Caliber/Gauge:	Action:
Barrel Length (end to end):	Finish:
Date Purchased:	From:
Price:	Paperwork:
Condition:	
Features:	

Accessories/Repairs		
Date	Description	Cost

Beneficiary:

Date Sold:	To:
Price:	Phone:
Condition:	Address:

Notes:

Photo of Firearm 20

Manufacturer & Model #:	Serial #:
Type: (circle one) Rifle Shotgun Handgun Other:	
Caliber/Gauge:	Action:
Barrel Length (end to end):	Finish:
Date Purchased:	From:
Price:	Paperwork:
Condition:	
Features:	

Accessories/Repairs		
Date	Description	Cost

Beneficiary:

Date Sold:	To:
Price:	Phone:
Condition:	Address:

Notes:

Photo of Firearm 21

Manufacturer & Model #:	Serial #:
Type: (circle one) Rifle Shotgun Handgun Other:	
Caliber/Gauge:	Action:
Barrel Length (end to end):	Finish:
Date Purchased:	From:
Price:	Paperwork:
Condition:	
Features:	

Accessories/Repairs		
Date	Description	Cost

Beneficiary:

Date Sold:	To:
Price:	Phone:
Condition:	Address:

Notes:

Photo of Firearm 22

Manufacturer & Model #:	Serial #:
Type: (circle one) Rifle Shotgun Handgun Other:	
Caliber/Gauge:	Action:
Barrel Length (end to end):	Finish:
Date Purchased:	From:
Price:	Paperwork:
Condition:	
Features:	

Accessories/Repairs		
Date	Description	Cost

Beneficiary:

Date Sold:	To:
Price:	Phone:
Condition:	Address:

Notes:

Photo of Firearm 23

Manufacturer & Model #:	Serial #:
Type: (circle one) Rifle Shotgun Handgun Other:	
Caliber/Gauge:	Action:
Barrel Length (end to end):	Finish:
Date Purchased:	From:
Price:	Paperwork:
Condition:	
Features:	

Accessories/Repairs		
Date	Description	Cost

Beneficiary:

Date Sold:	To:
Price:	Phone:
Condition:	Address:

Notes:

Photo of Firearm 24

Manufacturer & Model #:	Serial #:
Type: (circle one) Rifle Shotgun Handgun Other:	
Caliber/Gauge:	Action:
Barrel Length (end to end):	Finish:
Date Purchased:	From:
Price:	Paperwork:
Condition:	
Features:	

Accessories/Repairs		
Date	Description	Cost

Beneficiary:

Date Sold:	To:
Price:	Phone:
Condition:	Address:

Notes:

56

Photo of Firearm 25

Manufacturer & Model #:	Serial #:
Type: (circle one) Rifle Shotgun Handgun Other:	
Caliber/Gauge:	Action:
Barrel Length (end to end):	Finish:
Date Purchased:	From:
Price:	Paperwork:
Condition:	
Features:	

Accessories/Repairs		
Date	Description	Cost

Beneficiary:

Date Sold:	To:
Price:	Phone:
Condition:	Address:

Notes:

58

Photo of Firearm 26

Manufacturer & Model #:	Serial #:
Type: (circle one) Rifle Shotgun Handgun Other:	
Caliber/Gauge:	Action:
Barrel Length (end to end):	Finish:
Date Purchased:	From:
Price:	Paperwork:
Condition:	
Features:	

Accessories/Repairs		
Date	Description	Cost

Beneficiary:

Date Sold:	To:
Price:	Phone:
Condition:	Address:

Notes:

Photo of Firearm 27

Manufacturer & Model #:	Serial #:
Type: (circle one) Rifle Shotgun Handgun Other:	
Caliber/Gauge:	Action:
Barrel Length (end to end):	Finish:
Date Purchased:	From:
Price:	Paperwork:
Condition:	
Features:	

Accessories/Repairs		
Date	Description	Cost

Beneficiary:

Date Sold:	To:
Price:	Phone:
Condition:	Address:

Notes:

62

Photo of Firearm 28

Manufacturer & Model #:	Serial #:
Type: (circle one) Rifle Shotgun Handgun Other:	
Caliber/Gauge:	Action:
Barrel Length (end to end):	Finish:
Date Purchased:	From:
Price:	Paperwork:
Condition:	
Features:	

63

Accessories/Repairs		
Date	Description	Cost

Beneficiary:

Date Sold:	To:
Price:	Phone:
Condition:	Address:

Notes:

Photo of Firearm 29

Manufacturer & Model #:	Serial #:
Type: (circle one) Rifle Shotgun Handgun Other:	
Caliber/Gauge:	Action:
Barrel Length (end to end):	Finish:
Date Purchased:	From:
Price:	Paperwork:
Condition:	
Features:	

Accessories/Repairs		
Date	Description	Cost

Beneficiary:	
Date Sold:	To:
Price:	Phone:
Condition:	Address:

Notes:

Photo of Firearm 30

Manufacturer & Model #:	Serial #:
Type: (circle one) Rifle Shotgun Handgun Other:	
Caliber/Gauge:	Action:
Barrel Length (end to end):	Finish:
Date Purchased:	From:
Price:	Paperwork:
Condition:	
Features:	

Accessories/Repairs		
Date	Description	Cost

Beneficiary:

Date Sold:	To:
Price:	Phone:
Condition:	Address:

Notes:

Photo of Firearm 31

Manufacturer & Model #:	Serial #:
Type: (circle one) Rifle Shotgun Handgun Other:	
Caliber/Gauge:	Action:
Barrel Length (end to end):	Finish:
Date Purchased:	From:
Price:	Paperwork:
Condition:	
Features:	

Accessories/Repairs		
Date	Description	Cost

Beneficiary:	
Date Sold:	To:
Price:	Phone:
Condition:	Address:
Notes:	

Photo of Firearm 32

Manufacturer & Model #:	Serial #:
Type: (circle one) Rifle Shotgun Handgun Other:	
Caliber/Gauge:	Action:
Barrel Length (end to end):	Finish:
Date Purchased:	From:
Price:	Paperwork:
Condition:	
Features:	

Accessories/Repairs		
Date	Description	Cost

Beneficiary:

Date Sold:	To:
Price:	Phone:
Condition:	Address:

Notes:

Photo of Firearm 33

Manufacturer & Model #:	Serial #:
Type: (circle one) Rifle Shotgun Handgun Other:	
Caliber/Gauge:	Action:
Barrel Length (end to end):	Finish:
Date Purchased:	From:
Price:	Paperwork:
Condition:	
Features:	

Accessories/Repairs		
Date	Description	Cost

Beneficiary:

Date Sold:	To:
Price:	Phone:
Condition:	Address:

Notes:

74

Photo of Firearm 34

Manufacturer & Model #:	Serial #:
Type: (circle one) Rifle Shotgun Handgun Other:	
Caliber/Gauge:	Action:
Barrel Length (end to end):	Finish:
Date Purchased:	From:
Price:	Paperwork:
Condition:	
Features:	

Accessories/Repairs		
Date	Description	Cost

Beneficiary:	
Date Sold:	To:
Price:	Phone:
Condition:	Address:

Notes:

Photo of Firearm 35

Manufacturer & Model #:	Serial #:
Type: (circle one) Rifle Shotgun Handgun Other:	
Caliber/Gauge:	Action:
Barrel Length (end to end):	Finish:
Date Purchased:	From:
Price:	Paperwork:
Condition:	
Features:	

Accessories/Repairs		
Date	Description	Cost

Beneficiary:

Date Sold:	To:
Price:	Phone:
Condition:	Address:

Notes:

Photo of Firearm 36

Manufacturer & Model #:	Serial #:
Type: (circle one) Rifle Shotgun Handgun Other:	
Caliber/Gauge:	Action:
Barrel Length (end to end):	Finish:
Date Purchased:	From:
Price:	Paperwork:
Condition:	
Features:	

Accessories/Repairs		
Date	Description	Cost

Beneficiary:	
Date Sold:	To:
Price:	Phone:
Condition:	Address:

Notes:

Photo of Firearm 37

Manufacturer & Model #:	Serial #:
Type: (circle one) Rifle Shotgun Handgun Other:	
Caliber/Gauge:	Action:
Barrel Length (end to end):	Finish:
Date Purchased:	From:
Price:	Paperwork:
Condition:	
Features:	

Accessories/Repairs		
Date	Description	Cost

Beneficiary:	
Date Sold:	To:
Price:	Phone:
Condition:	Address:

Notes:

Photo of Firearm 38

Manufacturer & Model #:	Serial #:
Type: (circle one) Rifle Shotgun Handgun Other:	
Caliber/Gauge:	Action:
Barrel Length (end to end):	Finish:
Date Purchased:	From:
Price:	Paperwork:
Condition:	
Features:	

Accessories/Repairs		
Date	Description	Cost

Beneficiary:	
Date Sold:	To:
Price:	Phone:
Condition:	Address:

Notes:

Photo of Firearm 39

Manufacturer & Model #:	Serial #:
Type: (circle one) Rifle Shotgun Handgun Other:	
Caliber/Gauge:	Action:
Barrel Length (end to end):	Finish:
Date Purchased:	From:
Price:	Paperwork:
Condition:	
Features:	

Accessories/Repairs		
Date	Description	Cost

Beneficiary:

Date Sold:	To:
Price:	Phone:
Condition:	Address:

Notes:

Photo of Firearm 40

Manufacturer & Model #:	Serial #:
Type: (circle one) Rifle Shotgun Handgun Other:	
Caliber/Gauge:	Action:
Barrel Length (end to end):	Finish:
Date Purchased:	From:
Price:	Paperwork:
Condition:	
Features:	

Accessories/Repairs		
Date	Description	Cost

Beneficiary:

Date Sold:	To:
Price:	Phone:
Condition:	Address:

Notes:

Photo of Firearm 41

Manufacturer & Model #:	Serial #:
Type: (circle one) Rifle Shotgun Handgun Other:	
Caliber/Gauge:	Action:
Barrel Length (end to end):	Finish:
Date Purchased:	From:
Price:	Paperwork:
Condition:	
Features:	

Accessories/Repairs		
Date	Description	Cost

Beneficiary:	
Date Sold:	To:
Price:	Phone:
Condition:	Address:
Notes:	

Photo of Firearm 42

Manufacturer & Model #:	Serial #:
Type: (circle one) Rifle Shotgun Handgun Other:	
Caliber/Gauge:	Action:
Barrel Length (end to end):	Finish:
Date Purchased:	From:
Price:	Paperwork:
Condition:	
Features:	

Accessories/Repairs		
Date	Description	Cost

Beneficiary:	
Date Sold:	To:
Price:	Phone:
Condition:	Address:
Notes:	

Photo of Firearm 43

Manufacturer & Model #:	Serial #:
Type: (circle one) Rifle Shotgun Handgun Other:	
Caliber/Gauge:	Action:
Barrel Length (end to end):	Finish:
Date Purchased:	From:
Price:	Paperwork:
Condition:	
Features:	

Accessories/Repairs		
Date	Description	Cost

Beneficiary:

Date Sold:	To:
Price:	Phone:
Condition:	Address:

Notes:

Photo of Firearm 44

Manufacturer & Model #:	Serial #:
Type: (circle one) Rifle Shotgun Handgun Other:	
Caliber/Gauge:	Action:
Barrel Length (end to end):	Finish:
Date Purchased:	From:
Price:	Paperwork:
Condition:	
Features:	

Accessories/Repairs		
Date	Description	Cost

Beneficiary:

Date Sold:	To:
Price:	Phone:
Condition:	Address:

Notes:

Photo of Firearm 45

Manufacturer & Model #:	Serial #:
Type: (circle one) Rifle Shotgun Handgun Other:	
Caliber/Gauge:	Action:
Barrel Length (end to end):	Finish:
Date Purchased:	From:
Price:	Paperwork:
Condition:	
Features:	

Accessories/Repairs		
Date	Description	Cost

Beneficiary:

Date Sold:	To:
Price:	Phone:
Condition:	Address:

Notes:

Photo of Firearm 46

Manufacturer & Model #:	Serial #:
Type: (circle one) Rifle Shotgun Handgun Other:	
Caliber/Gauge:	Action:
Barrel Length (end to end):	Finish:
Date Purchased:	From:
Price:	Paperwork:
Condition:	
Features:	

Accessories/Repairs		
Date	Description	Cost

Beneficiary:

Date Sold:	To:
Price:	Phone:
Condition:	Address:

Notes:

Photo of Firearm 47

Manufacturer & Model #:	Serial #:
Type: (circle one) Rifle Shotgun Handgun Other:	
Caliber/Gauge:	Action:
Barrel Length (end to end):	Finish:
Date Purchased:	From:
Price:	Paperwork:
Condition:	
Features:	

Accessories/Repairs		
Date	Description	Cost

Beneficiary:	
Date Sold:	To:
Price:	Phone:
Condition:	Address:

Notes:

Photo of Firearm 48

Manufacturer & Model #:	Serial #:
Type: (circle one) Rifle Shotgun Handgun Other:	
Caliber/Gauge:	Action:
Barrel Length (end to end):	Finish:
Date Purchased:	From:
Price:	Paperwork:
Condition:	
Features:	

Accessories/Repairs		
Date	Description	Cost

Beneficiary:

Date Sold:	To:
Price:	Phone:
Condition:	Address:

Notes:

Photo of Firearm 49

Manufacturer & Model #:	Serial #:
Type: (circle one) Rifle Shotgun Handgun Other:	
Caliber/Gauge:	Action:
Barrel Length (end to end):	Finish:
Date Purchased:	From:
Price:	Paperwork:
Condition:	
Features:	

Accessories/Repairs		
Date	Description	Cost

Beneficiary:

Date Sold:	To:
Price:	Phone:
Condition:	Address:

Notes:

Photo of Firearm 50

Manufacturer & Model #:	Serial #:
Type: (circle one) Rifle Shotgun Handgun Other:	
Caliber/Gauge:	Action:
Barrel Length (end to end):	Finish:
Date Purchased:	From:
Price:	Paperwork:
Condition:	
Features:	

Accessories/Repairs		
Date	Description	Cost

Beneficiary:

Date Sold:	To:
Price:	Phone:
Condition:	Address:

Notes:

The Second Amendment

The Second Amendment of the United States Constitution reads: "A well regulated Militia, being necessary to the security of a free State, the right of the people to keep and bear Arms, shall not be infringed." Such language has created considerable debate regarding the Amendment's intended scope. On the one hand, some believe that the Amendment's phrase "the right of the people to keep and bear Arms" creates an individual constitutional right for citizens of the United States. Under this "individual right theory," the United States Constitution restricts legislative bodies from prohibiting firearm possession, or at the very least, the Amendment renders prohibitory and restrictive regulation presumptively unconstitutional. On the other hand, some scholars point to the prefatory language "a well regulated Militia" to argue that the Framers intended only to restrict Congress from legislating away a state's right to self-defense. Scholars have come to call this theory "the collective rights theory." A collective rights theory of the Second Amendment asserts that citizens do not have an individual right to possess guns and that local, state, and federal legislative bodies therefore possess the authority to regulate firearms without implicating a constitutional right.

In 1939 the U.S. Supreme Court considered the matter in *United States v. Miller*. 307 U.S. 174. The Court adopted a collective rights approach in this case, determining that Congress could regulate a sawed-off shotgun that had moved in interstate commerce under the National Firearms Act of 1934 because the evidence did not suggest that the shotgun "has some reasonable relationship to the preservation or efficiency of a well regulated milita . . . ." The Court then explained that the Framers included the Second Amendment to ensure the effectiveness of the military.

This precedent stood for nearly 70 years when in 2008 the U.S. Supreme Court revisited the issue in the case of *District of Columbia v. Heller* (07-290). The plaintiff in HELLER challenged the constitutionality of the Washington D.C. handgun ban, a statute that had stood for 32 years. Many considered the statute the most stringent in the nation. In a 5-4 decision, the Court, meticulously detailing the history and tradition of the Second Amendment at the time of the Constitutional Convention, proclaimed that the Second Amendment established an individual right for U.S. citizens to possess firearms and struck down the D.C. handgun ban as violative of that right. The majority carved out MILLER as an exception to the general rule that Americans may possess firearms, claiming that law-abiding citizens cannot use sawed-off shotguns for any law-abiding purchase. Similarly, the Court in its dicta found regulations of similar weaponry that cannot be used for law-abiding purchases as laws that would not implicate the Second Amendment. Further, the Court suggested that the United States Constitution would not disallow regulations prohibiting criminals and the mentally ill from firearm possession.

Thus, the Supreme Court has revitalized the Second Amendment. The Court continued to strengthen the Second Amendment through the 2010 decision in MCDONALD V. CITY OF CHICAGO (08-1521). The plaintiff in MCDONALD challenged the constitutionally of the Chicago handgun ban, which prohibited handgun possession by almost all private citizens. In a 5-4 decisions, the Court, citing the intentions of the framers and ratifiers of the Fourteenth Amendment, held that the Second Amendment applies to the states through the incorporation doctrine. However, the Court did not have a majority on which clause of the Fourteenth Amendment incorporates the fundamental right to keep and bear arms for the purpose of self-defense. While Justice Alito and his supporters looked to the Due Process Clause, Justice Thomas in his concurrence stated that the Privileges and Immunities Clause should justify incorporation.

However, several questions still remain unanswered, such as whether regulations less stringent than the D.C. statute implicate the Second Amendment, whether lower courts will apply their dicta regarding permissible restrictions, and what level of scrutiny the courts should apply when analyzing a statute that infringes on the Second Amendment.

Recent case law since HELLER suggests that courts are willing to, for example, uphold

- regulations which ban weapons on government property. US v Dorosan, 350 Fed. Appx. 874 (5th Cir. 2009) (upholding defendant's conviction for bringing a handgun onto post office property);

- regulations which ban the illegal possession of a handgun as a juvenile, convicted felon. US v Rene, 583 F.3d 8 (1st Cir. 2009) (holding that the Juvenile Delinquency Act ban of juvenile possession of handguns did not violate the Second Amendment);

- regulations which require a permit to carry concealed weapon. Kachalsky v County of Westchester, 701 F.3d 81 (2nd Cir. 2012) (holding that a New York law preventing individuals from obtaining a license to possess a concealed firearm in public for general purposes unless the individual showed proper cause did not violate the Second Amendment.)

The Four Cardinal Rules of Firearm Safety

1. Treat all guns as if they are always loaded

2. Always point the muzzle in a safe direction; never let your muzzle cover anything that you are not willing to kill

3. Keep your finger off the trigger until you are on target and prepared to fire

4. Be sure of your target, its surroundings, and what is beyond it; never shoot at anything that you have not positively identified.

FastForwardPublishing.com

Made in the USA
Monee, IL
24 February 2021

61238371R00063